The HAPPY Doodle Book

Taro Gomi

chronicle books · san francisco

Doodling is best when you're happy and having fun. And the more you **doodle,** the happier you'll be!

How does your face look when you're happy?

**Draw a face for this
cheerful frog.**

What's inside this box of fun?

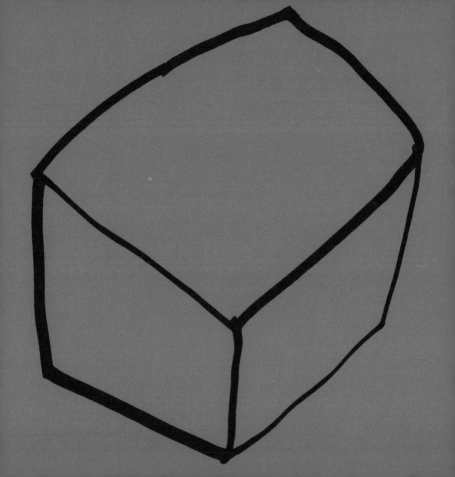

What silly things will you put on this hat?

Let's draw lots of playful chicks.

**Draw a smiling person
in this house.**

What kind of clothes do you wear when you're happy?

**Draw some hands for
this jolly clock.**

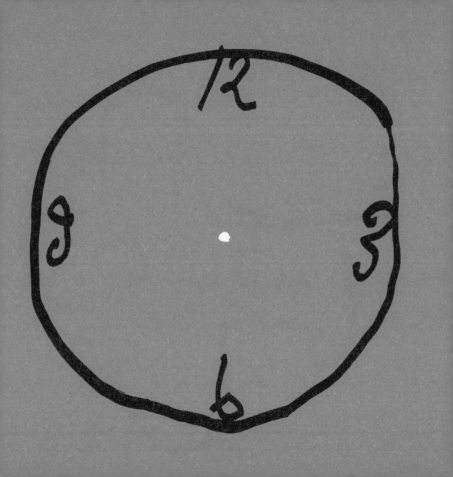

Let's make these airplanes look silly.

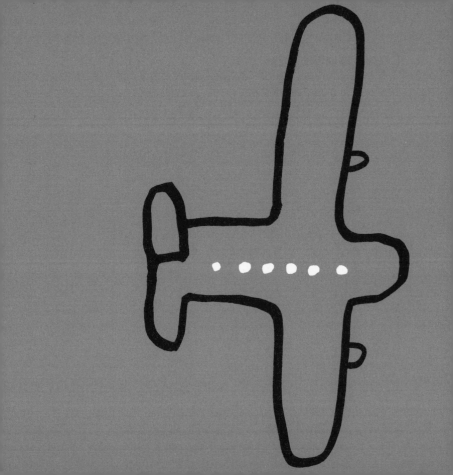

Decorate this cheerful cake.

Let's draw an
exciting car.

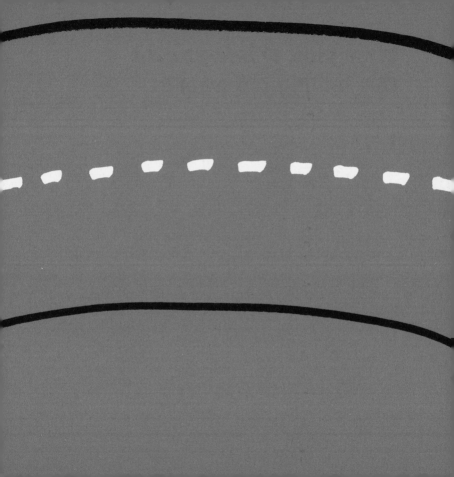

What kind of bow should this smiling girl wear?

Let's draw lots of little birds.

Let's draw a laughing snowman.

**Draw someone happily
riding the bicycle.**

Let's draw a cheery
feeling on the T-shirt.

What kind of shoes
are joyful shoes?

Let's do some delightful math.

$$\begin{array}{r} 5\overset{6}{4} \\ + \\ \hline \end{array}$$

Draw a person playfully kicking the ball.

Let's draw some jubilant flowers.

Merrily draw the letter A.

**Let's make
Mr. Robot laugh.**

What kind of umbrella does a happy person carry?

Let's draw a busy beach.

What kind of face will you give this happy rabbit?

Isn't doodling lots of fun? Turn the page to doodle more!

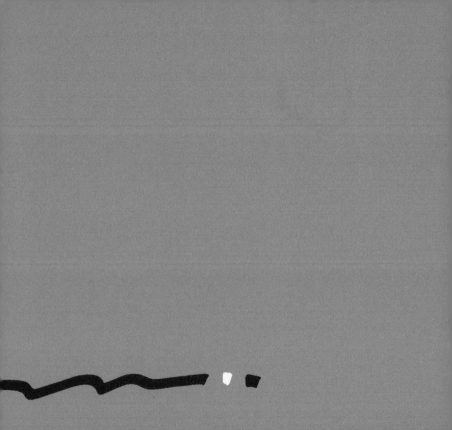

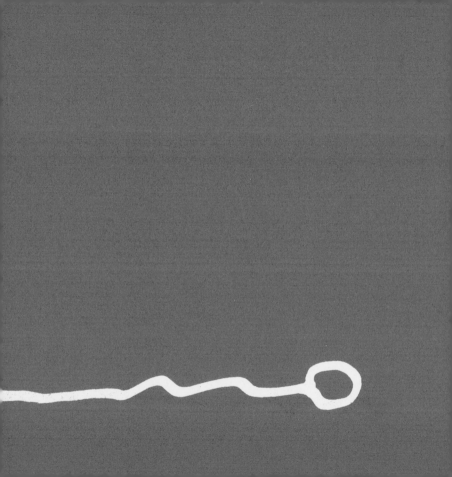

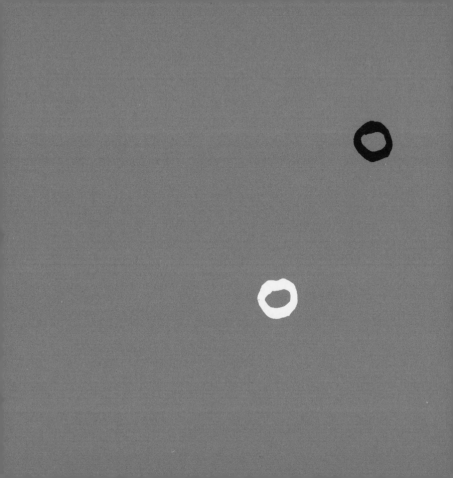

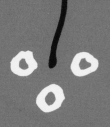

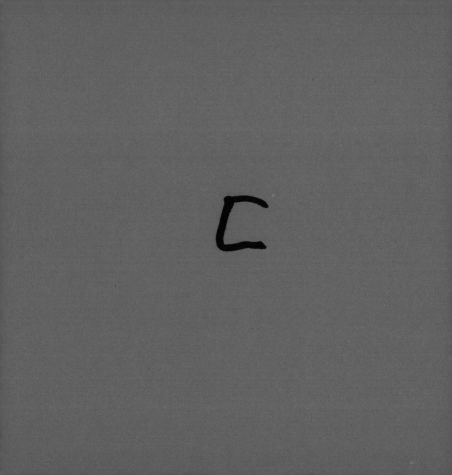

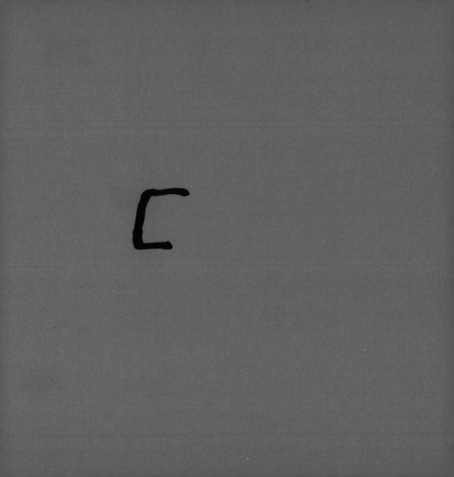

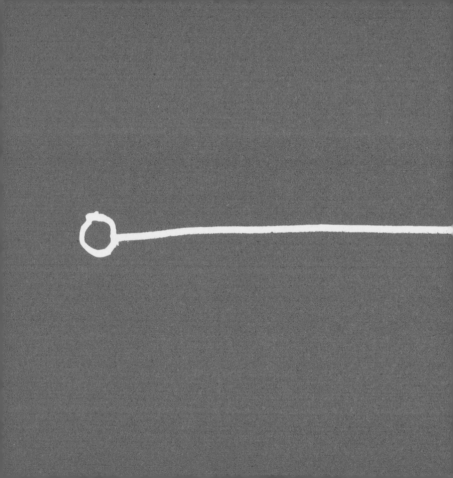

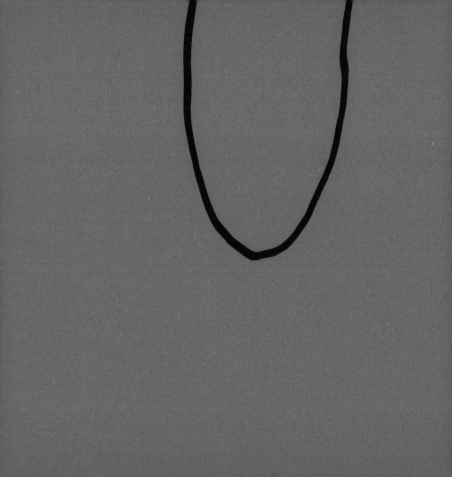

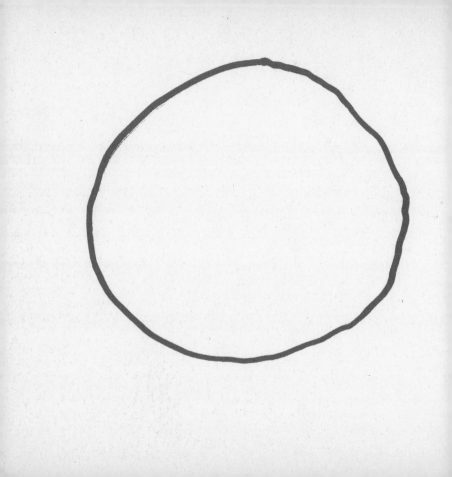

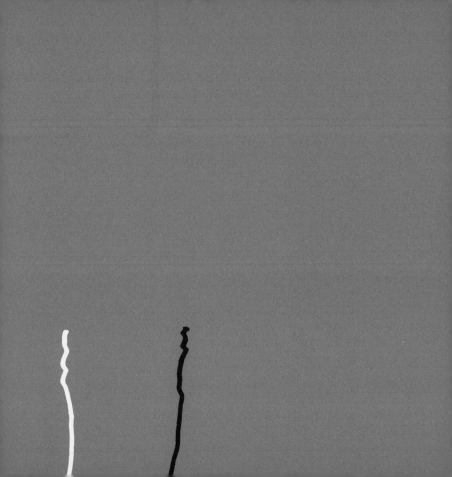

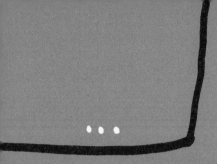

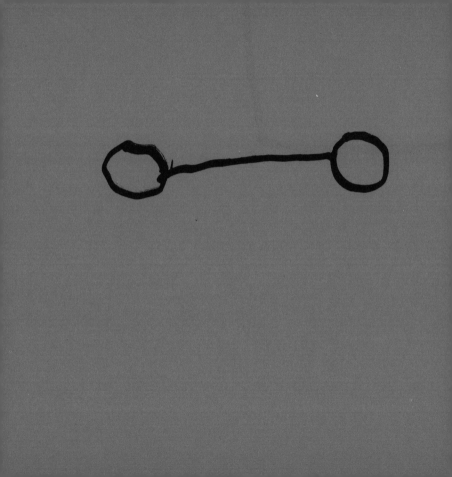

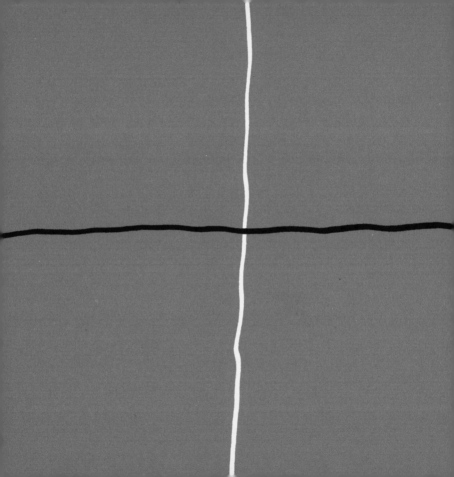

Who is climbing?

These are bookshelves.

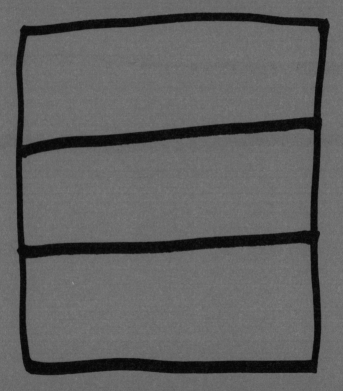

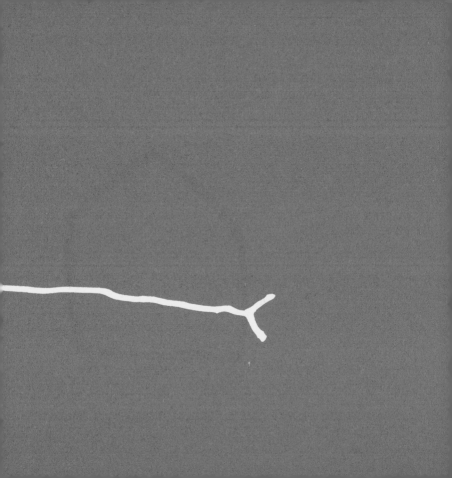

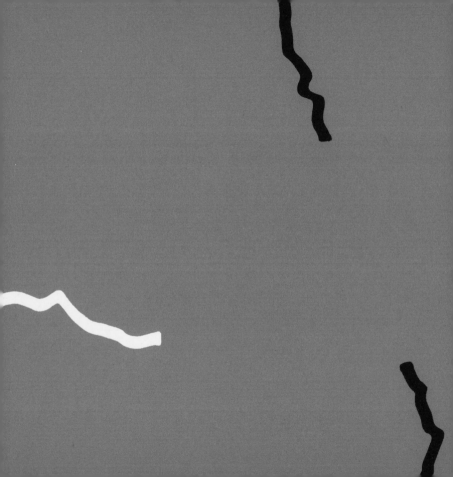

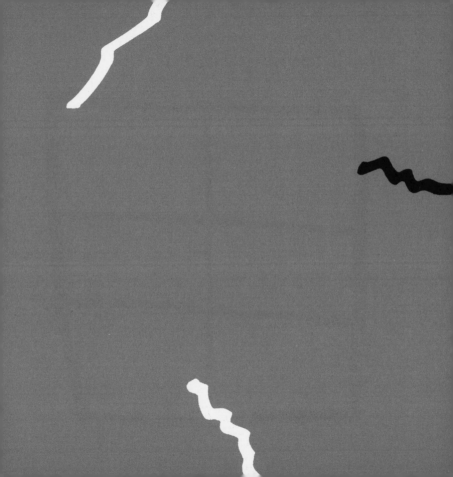

Who is looking out the **window?**

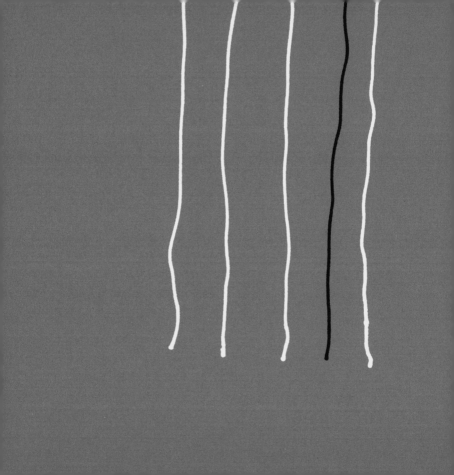

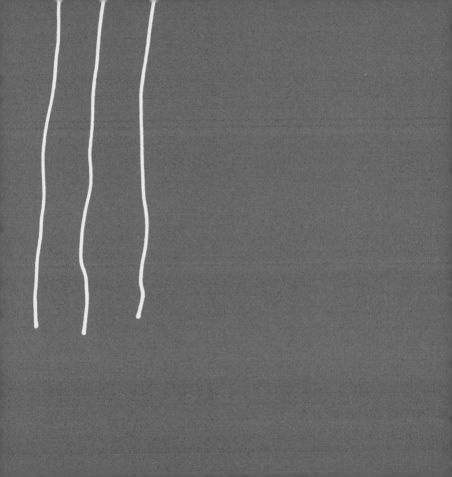

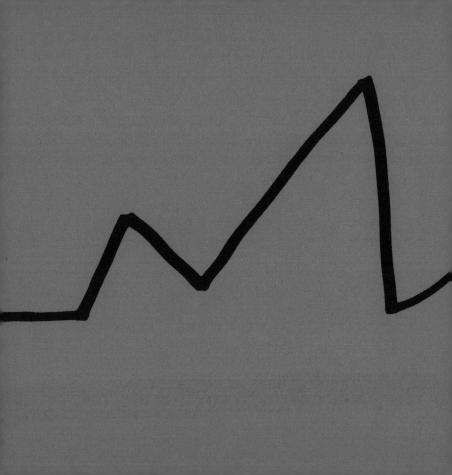

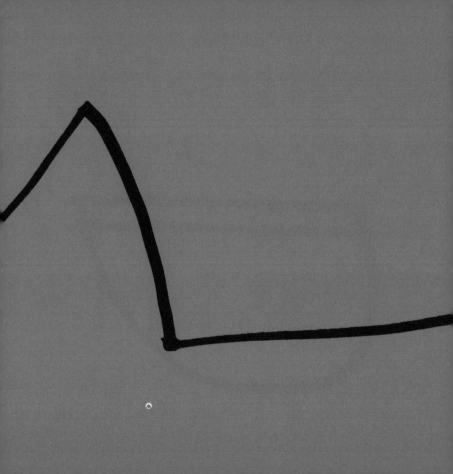

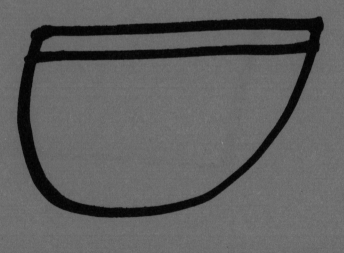

**Someone is peeking
out of the hole!**

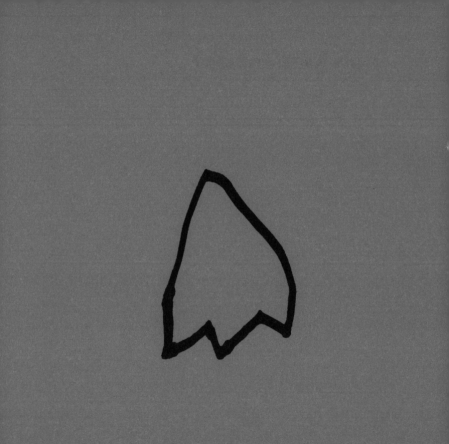

Is this Miss Rabbit?

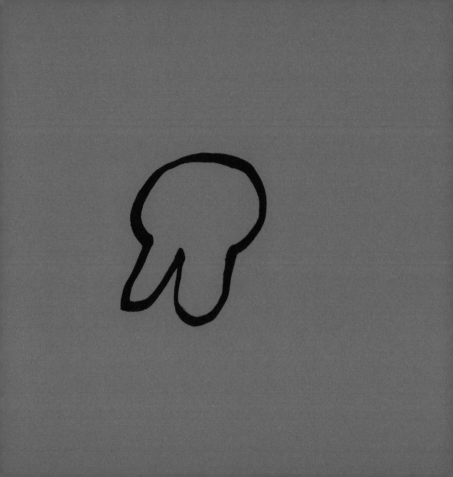

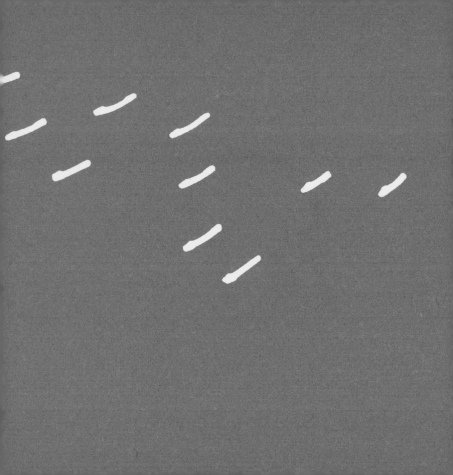

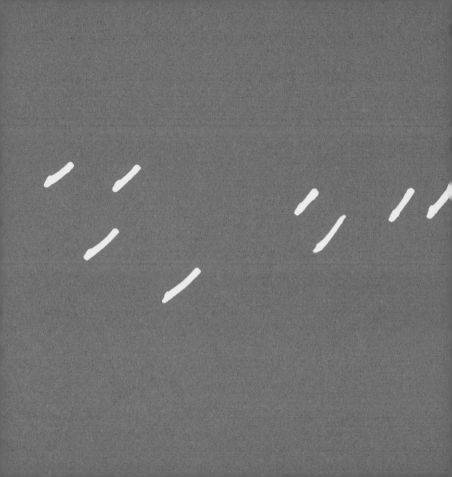

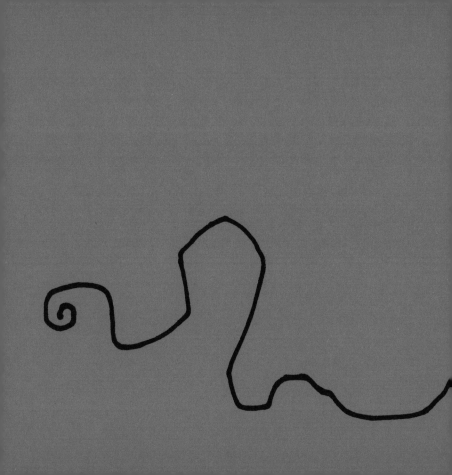

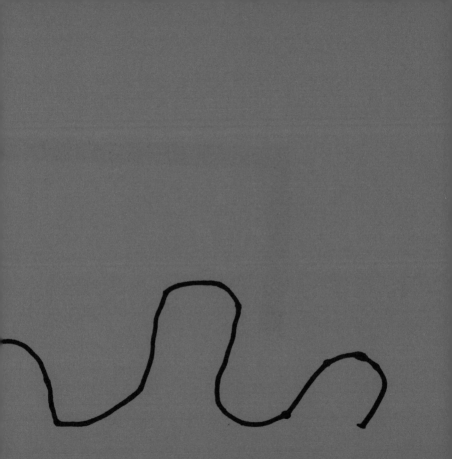

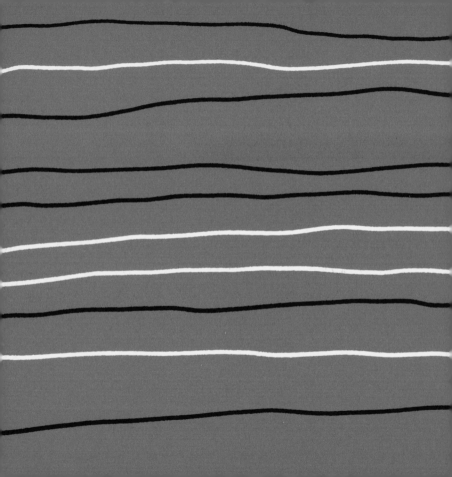

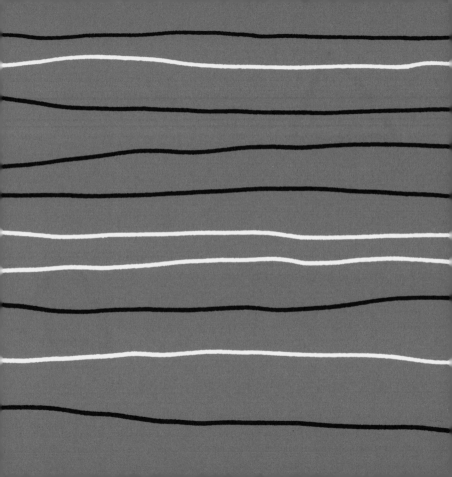

A ghost!

Another ghost!

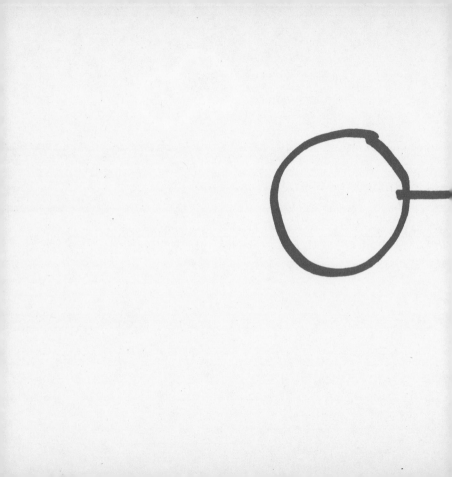

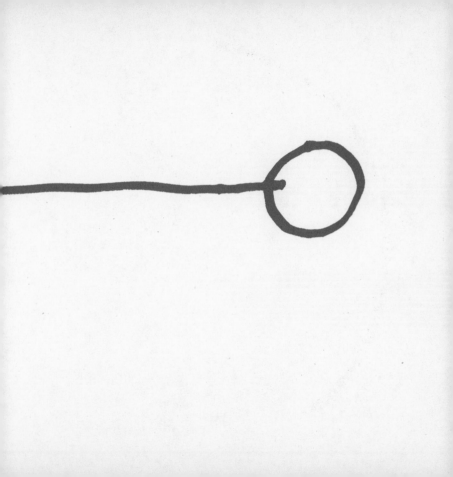

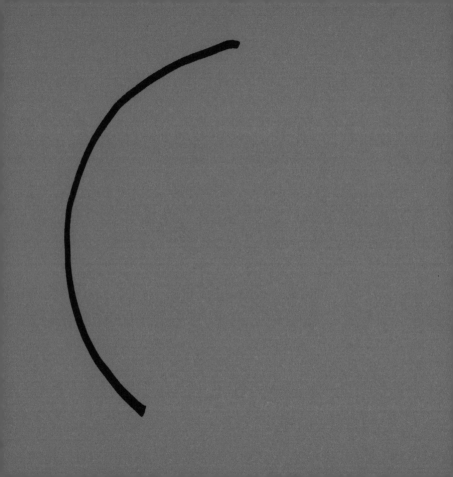

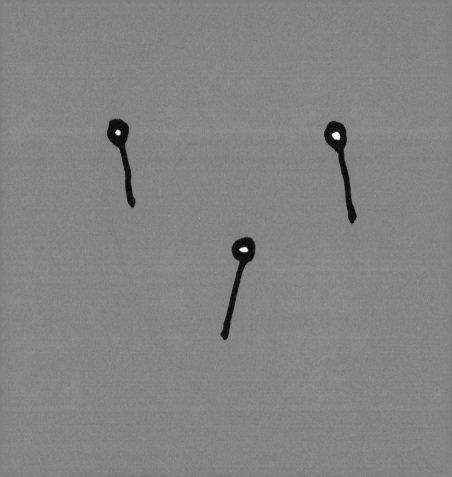

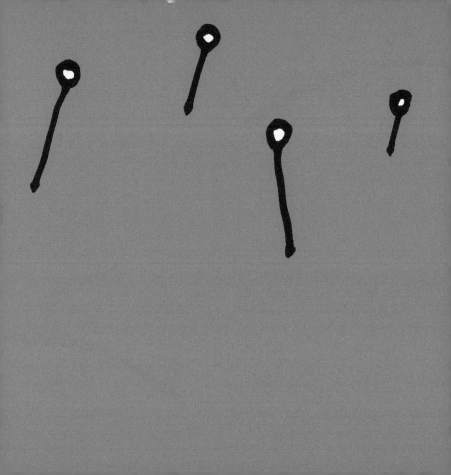

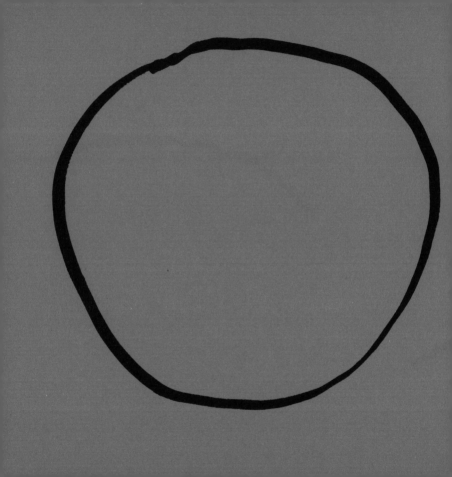

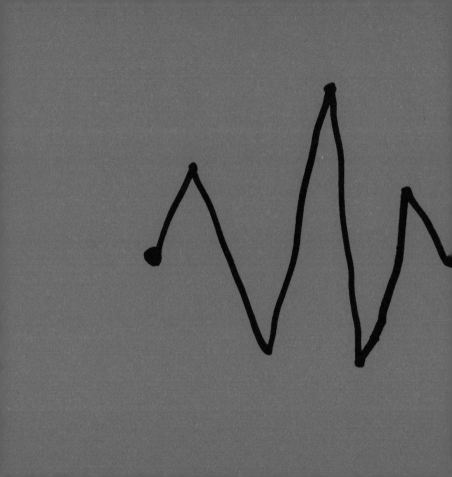

Please draw even smaller things.

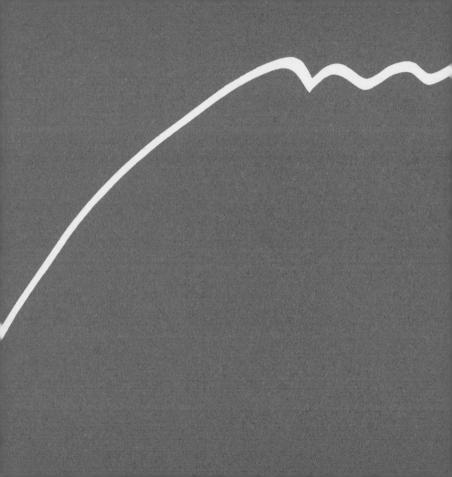

Look! Someone is sliding down the hill!

Someone is coming!

Are these numbers?

Are these bananas?

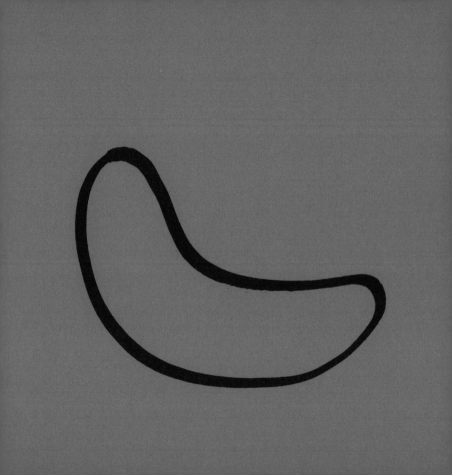

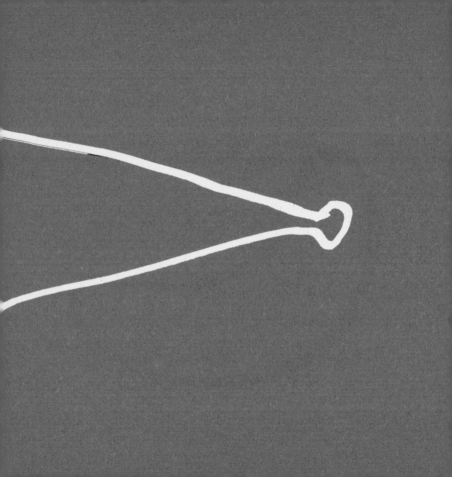

Who is going up the stairs?

Who is coming down the stairs?

**Oh, look.
The moon!**

Where is his mother?

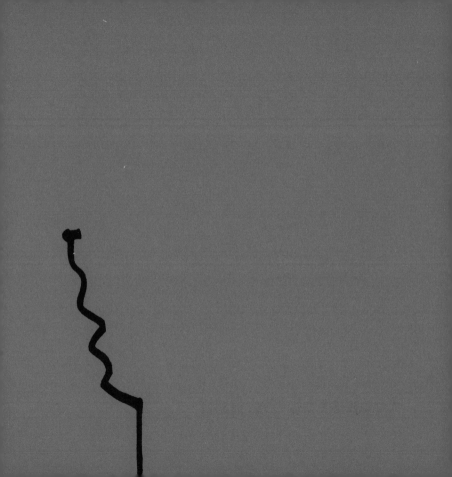

Look at all the fish!

Are these bubbles?

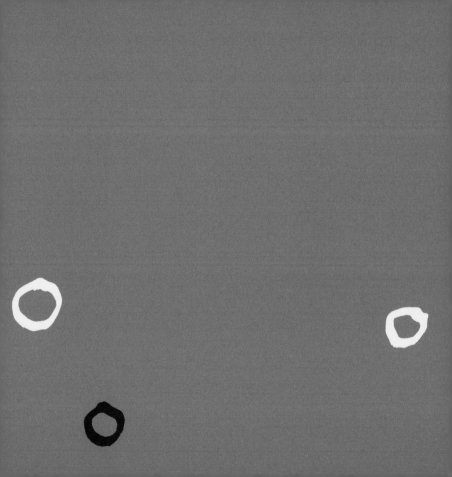

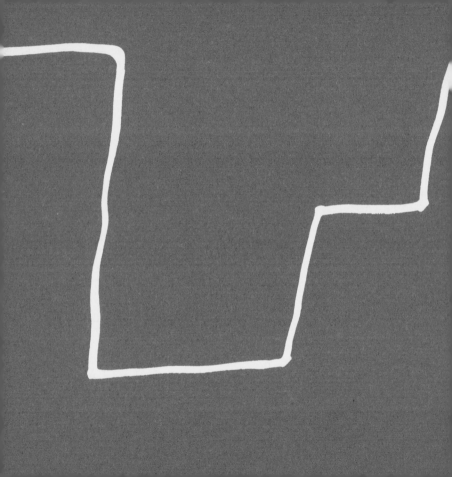

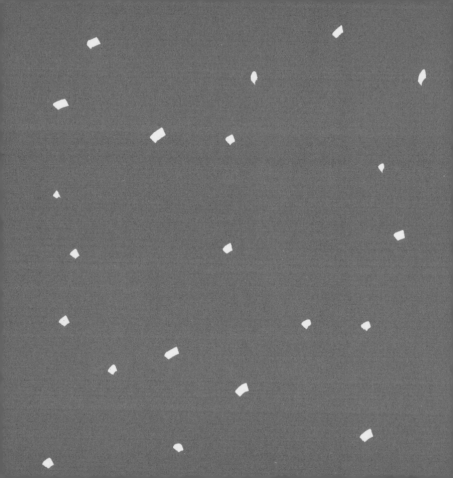

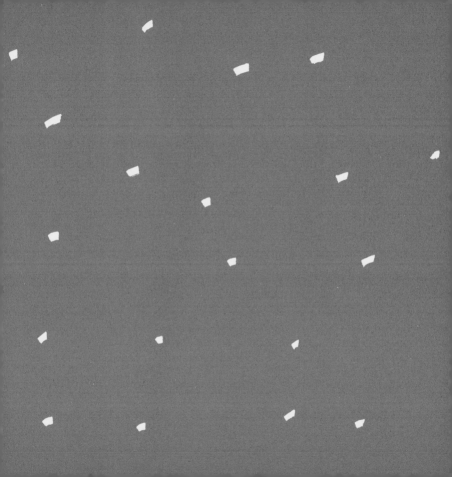

Are these fireworks?

What's inside?

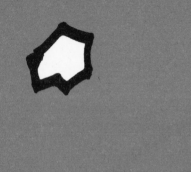

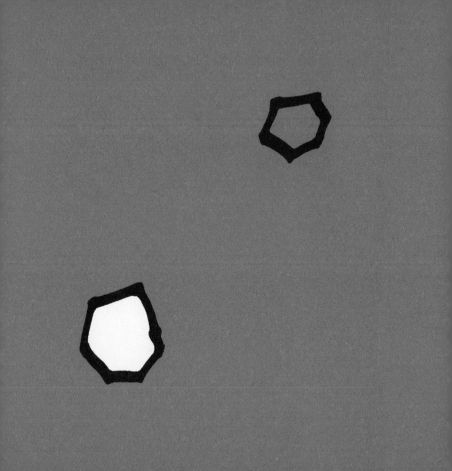

What are these shaggy things?

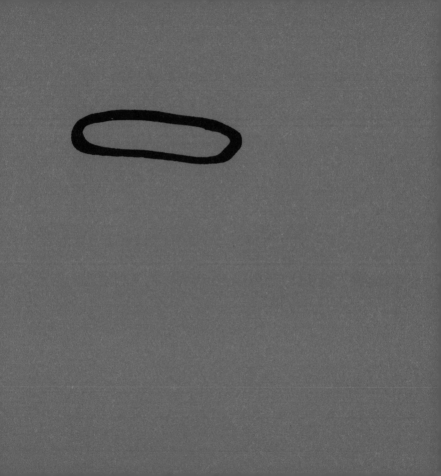

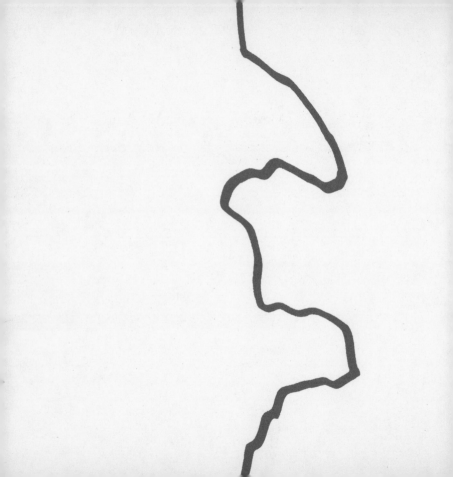

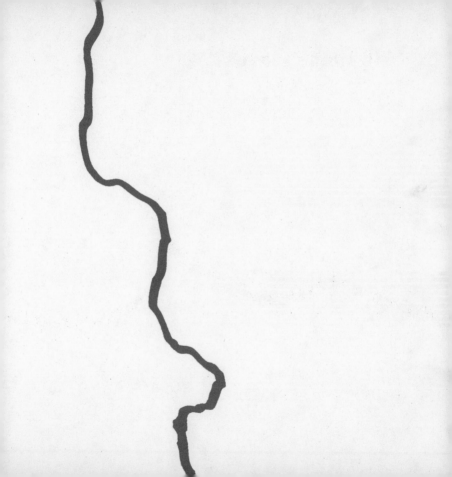

Are these waves?

Is this a cloud?

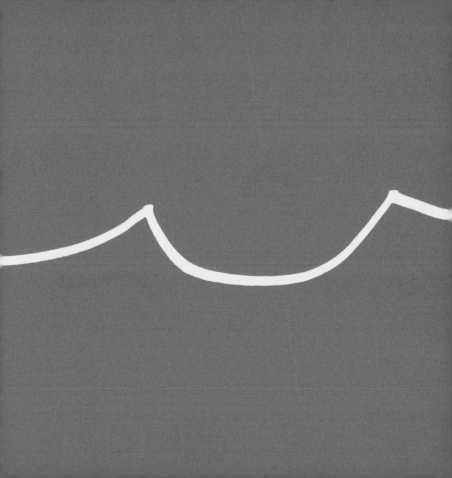

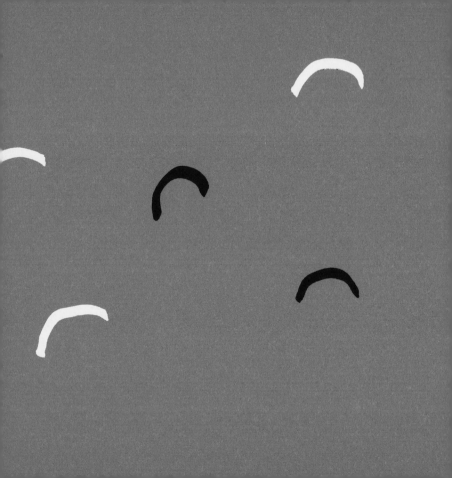

**What's on
these hands?**

What kind of flower do you like?

Doodling is always lots of fun. Let's **doodle** again!

Original edition published in Japan by BRONZE PUBLISHING Inc., Tokyo,
under the title *Ureshii Tokino Rakugaki Book*. Copyright © 2010 Taro Gomi.

First United States edition published in 2012 by Chronicle Books LLC.
English text copyright © 2012 by Chronicle Books LLC.
All rights reserved.

ISBN 978-1-4521-0780-6

Manufactured in Singapore.
Typeset in Avenir.

1 3 5 7 9 10 8 6 4 2

Chronicle Books LLC
680 Second Street, San Francisco, California 94107
www.chroniclekids.com